MONSTERS

**Richard Haycraft and
Nicholas Luxmoore**

HODDER AND STOUGHTON

LONDON SYDNEY AUCKLAND TORONTO

YOU MONSTER!

When they are cross, some parents call their children 'monsters', but what do they mean? Do they know what a monster is?

They probably say the word 'monster' because they think that a monster is a noisy, messy, selfish thing, and that their child is behaving like one. But what is a monster?

1 Think of someone you know.
2 Think of what they are like.
3 Think of *one* word to describe them.

The word you have chosen describes them in a very simple way, but of course there is much more you can say, and the more you say, the more you describe them. It would be unfair to think that your word sums them up all the time. Nobody behaves like a monster all the time.

Write down the word you chose to describe the person you know.

Next, plan and write a full and detailed description of them. Think of the ways they behave. Think of the ways they feel. Think of the ways they think and the things they say. Think of lots of words that describe them truthfully.

The job of a dictionary is to explain the meaning of each word we use. Sometimes two dictionaries explain the same word in two slightly different ways. This is what two dictionaries say about the word 'monster':

1 an ugly creature or plant
2 a huge, imaginary, cruel thing

If you ask people what the word 'monster' means, different people will give different explanations. Some people will not know what the dictionary says the word means. Sometimes we use words without really understanding what they mean.

Here are four examples of words we use to describe other people, and the dictionary explanation of what the words mean. Two of the words have more than one meaning according to the dictionary.

Fool: a person whose job was to tell jokes to kings and queens; or a pudding made with cream or custard; or a silly person.

Cretin: a mentally backward dwarf with wide-set eyes, a broad flat nose and a tongue that sticks out.

Madman: a foolish or careless person; or someone who behaves violently; or someone who is insane.

Gypsy: a member of a wandering tribe now living in Europe and North America who centuries ago used to live in north-west India.

To test whether people outside your class really know what they mean when they use these four words and the word 'monster', try asking them.

It might be best to use a tape recorder, but with only paper and a pen you will still be able to make notes.

Ask them what exactly each word means and make a note of what they say. Don't tell them what the dictionary says until afterwards.

When you have finished questioning people, use your notes to write a careful description of what they said to you.

If you can, try to explain why you think they answered the way they did.

The green thing

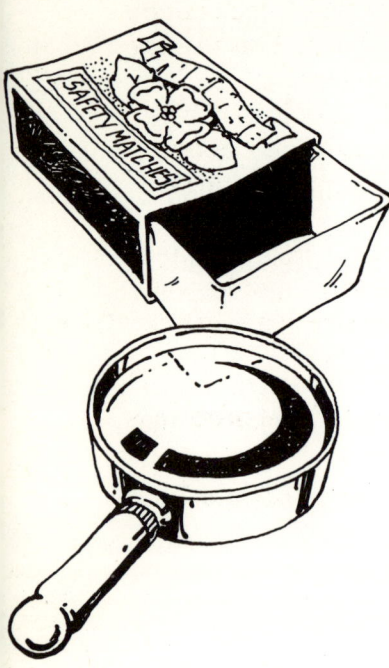

Jack found it in the garden, early one morning when the day is new and life itself is being reborn. At first he thought it was an ordinary caterpillar, until it looked at him with a tiny, green, human face. He could hardly believe his eyes. He picked it up, put it in a match-box, and took it up to his room. There he examined it through a magnifying-glass.

No, he hadn't imagined the phenomenon. It was a caterpillar with a minute human head, bald as a baby's or an old man's. It had no eyebrows or eyelashes but a few little whiskers on its chin. White whiskers. Its eyes were jade green, bright and intelligent. The skin of its face was as green as its caterpillar body. With a pin, Jack gently prised open its minuscule mouth. It had tiny, tiny, brilliantly green teeth.

It was very strange, of course but it had a *nice* face – a gentle, friendly expression. Could it speak?

'Hello. Good morning,' Jack said to it.

It made no sound but shook its little head slightly, as if in apology for not being able to respond.

'Never mind. Don't worry,' Jack consoled it. 'You're a new little thing for this world, aren't you? Are you the first?' It nodded. 'I'll look after you,' Jack promised.

He broke a cabbage leaf into small pieces and put them in the match-box with the little creature, so it could have a meal. Then he made a hole in the box, big enough for it to see out, but not for it to crawl out. He didn't want to lose it.

He left it on his bedroom window-sill, so that it could look out of the window if it got bored while he was at school. He didn't mention it to his parents. It was his secret.

When he returned home after school that day, he went immediately to see how it was getting on. He set the magnifying glass over its little face and the green eyes blinked a 'hello'. He wondered what it was thinking. Did caterpillars think? Maybe not ordinary ones, but this was a person-caterpillar. How small its brain must be in that tiny bald head! All those millions of cells crammed together. He named it Ben.

A few days later he noticed that it was growing. It was too big for the match-box already, so he gave it a new home – an old chocolate-box which he furnished with greenery, and another hole for Ben to look out of. Its dependence on him made him love it. This was the first time any creature had relied on him.

His mother noticed the box when she cleaned his room, but didn't look inside. She was usually decent that way. She didn't nose into Jack's things, unless anything smelled, and Ben didn't.

Indeed, all would have been well for Jack and his new pet if Ben had stayed the same size – but he went on growing. Soon he was nearly the size of a squirrel.

The green thing has started growing. What problems will Jack have looking after it?

What problems will he have when other people find out about it?

What do you think will happen next?

Jack's father had some books delivered, so Jack commandeered the big box they arrived in. This provided Ben with a suitable home, and everything was fine – until the day when his mother was cleaning his room and Ben looked out at her through his 'window' in the box. She screamed like some daft woman watching a horror film. Luckily Jack was in the house as the school had been closed for the day for roof repairs, and he dashed upstairs, guessing the worst.

With a white face turning rapidly red, she demanded: 'Jack! *What* is in that box?'

'It's only Ben,' he explained calmly to his shaking mother. 'He's a sort of big caterpillar with a person inside him, and the person-part shows in his head. He's my friend – he's ever so gentle. Come and say hello to him.' He opened the lid of the box. His mother caught his hand, slammed the lid down again, bundled him out of the room in front of her, and closed and locked the door. Pocketing the key, she tore down to the telephone and rang his father at work. Jack felt ashamed of her. What a display! He could hear her voice in fragments: 'A green thing – a monster in the house – you must come!'

Later his father came. 'What's all this about a monster in the house?' he asked his wife. 'If you've dragged me away from the office for nothing –'

'Go and look in Jack's room and you'll see.' She passed him the key.

'Ben isn't a monster. He's a bit bigger than he was, that's all,' said Jack, following his father up the stairs. 'He's got a good face, quite a religious look really.'

They went into the bedroom.

'Well, where is it?'

'In your old book-box.'

His father looked inside. Ben looked back at him and gave a friendly little smile with his green teeth.

'You see?' said Jack. 'He likes us. Mum's making a fuss about nothing. Anyone would think I'd brought a gorilla into the house the way she carried on, or the Loch Ness monster, or something.'

'It's macabre,' said his father, who had turned greenish.

'Ben is *not* macabre! Oh, you're rotten! Just because he isn't exactly like us, you condemn him. That's prejudice.'

'Where did you find it?'

'In the garden. He was only tiny then. He's grown with my care and attention. He's no trouble.'

'I think it's a police matter,' muttered his father.

'Police! Ben's done nothing wrong! He behaves better than most people. What are you doing? Oh, Dad, please . . .'

His father closed the box, picked it up, carried it down to the car and drove away with it. Jack was frantic. 'Poor Ben – poor Ben – what'll they do to him?'

'If they've got any sense, they'll destroy it,' said his mother.

'Why?' shouted Jack. 'Because he was born the way he is? If he's got funny genes, can he help it? I'll bet if you'd been born with a caterpillar-body you'd be pretty sick if people called you a monster and threatened to kill you . . .'

'Shut up, shut up, shut up,' said his mother.

Jack shut up.

Why do Jack's parents feel the way they do?

What do you think they'll do?

His father returned later, without the box. 'They're going to look into it,' he said. 'It's out of our hands now, thank heavens.' He refused to discuss the matter further.

Jack had an almost sleepless night, worrying about Ben. In the morning he behaved with cunning quietness. He set out at the usual time for school, but went to the police station instead. He gave his name to the constable at the reception desk and added: 'My father brought a friend of mine called Ben here yesterday. I gather you kept him in custody. I want to know what's going to happen to him.'

'Oh, you're the kid who found the green thing, are you?' said the policeman. 'We've been in touch with the RSPCA. They're sending someone.'

'Please may I see Ben?'

'I don't see why not.' He took Jack to a cell where Ben was sitting quietly in his box, surrounded by greenery, and looking, in Jack's eyes, charming and endearing.

'I'm glad to see you're feeding him O.K.,' said Jack.

'Oh, yes. Between you and me, I've quite taken to him. He's a peaceful little chap, not like some we've had in this cell – drunks, vandals, layabouts.'

'Ben has good manners. They're natural to him,' said Jack. 'But just because he's different, my parents can't stand him.'

'Some people are scared of the unusual,' nodded the constable. 'In the force, we're dealing with unusual things all the time, so nothing seems overly strange to us. He seems to be growing rather fast though. He's put on a bit overnight.'

Although Ben couldn't speak, he seemed to understand what they were saying, for he gave a modest, green-toothed smile, as if he were proud of his rate of development.

'It doesn't matter about him growing,' said Jack. 'It's not as if he has to wear clothes to grow out of.'

'No, but if he gets bigger and bigger . . .'

'But things don't. Even elephants and whales stop sometime. Anyway. I think there's room in the world for every sort of creature and it's time we had some new ones. Ben is the first of a new sort. Ben the First.'

The man from the RSPCA arrived, cheerful and red-bearded. 'Well, where's this green thing then? I say! What a quaint – er – person.'

'His name's Ben,' said Jack.

'Good morning, Ben,' said Red-beard.

Ben nodded politely.

'What's the problem then? No one's been cruel to him, have they?'

'No, but we don't know what to do with him,' said the policeman. 'Young Jack, here, found him, but his parents won't let him keep the creature at home, and we can't hold him here as if he were a criminal.'

'Then I suggest the zoo,' said the RSPCA man. 'How about it, Jack? He'd have a cage to himself, regular meals, lots of people to look at. Zoo animals love looking at people. Never a dull moment. The hyenas laugh fit to bust.'

'O.K.,' said Jack, hiding his disappointment. He was finding that if he was calm and self-controlled himself, other people seemed to behave better too. Yesterday he'd made his parents more upset by losing his temper. *Ben* knew how to behave. He was worth imitating.

Would you have let the green thing go to the zoo?

Red-beard rang the zoo and the three of them set off almost immediately, Red-beard and Jack, with Ben in his box. Luckily the car journey was soon over, as the zoological garden was part of the local park, and Red-beard seemed to know everyone there. After Ben had been examined by a vet, who wore a baffled expression as he signed the various official forms, Ben was placed in his new quarters. He had a cage to himself, lots of greenery to eat and climb about on, and a good view of the passing people. Except that they soon stopped passing and stood to stare. At first, a few laughed and pointed, or cried out and were scared, but there was something about Ben's serenity which eventually affected the crowd. They became a little more civilised under his steady green-eyed gaze.

A reporter from the local paper turned up, accompanied by a photographer, who took pictures of Ben, and of Jack and Ben together.

'It'll make an interesting feature,' said the reporter, 'and I'll bet we have a few boffins along to examine your discovery, Jack. Such a wise-looking head the creature's got, like some old sage who happens to have turned green. A Hindu monk, maybe? Perhaps in his former life he behaved badly, so he was reincarnated as a lower form of life – a caterpillar – but he managed to keep his head.' He chuckled. 'It's a novelty anyway.'

Novelty was the word. News of the zoo's new attraction soon circulated, and in the afternoon crowds began to arrive to see the person-caterpillar. Sellers of ice cream, iced lollies and hot-dogs made a small fortune.

Jack had a marvellous day, then went home in the early evening and explained to his parents that he'd been kept late at school for a sports practice.

This deceit could not be maintained, however, for soon the telephone began to ring. Pressmen, scientists, biologists, anthropologists, zoologists, psychiatrists, spiritualists, Buddhists, Hindus, parsons, pet-food manufacturers, Old Uncle Tom Cobley and all were ringing up to speak to Jack about Ben. Jack even coped with all this excitement without flapping, and his parents stopped being cross and looked with new respect at their son.

The initial clamour died down. Days passed. And Ben grew.

Soon he had to be moved to a larger cage – then to a larger one still. His body became almost elephantine and his head grew bigger than any ordinary human head. The huge green eyes were beautiful and compelling. Some of the zoo workers nicknamed him 'the green god'.

That was when the circus people got interested. Would the zoo authorities lend Ben to them for their summer show in the park? Could Jack ride on Ben's long, green back and control him in the ring? Easily, said Jack.

His parents protested a little, but the circus people quietened them with a very generous cheque, and they agreed that Jack might join the circus during his summer holiday and ride Ben in the ring.

Ben was hardly agile – caterpillars have small legs in comparison with the size of their bodies – but now he was so big all over, he could heave himself along at a reasonable rate, and he soon learned to nod politely from side to side, blink his beautiful jade eyes, and smile his glittering green-toothed smile at the cheering audience.

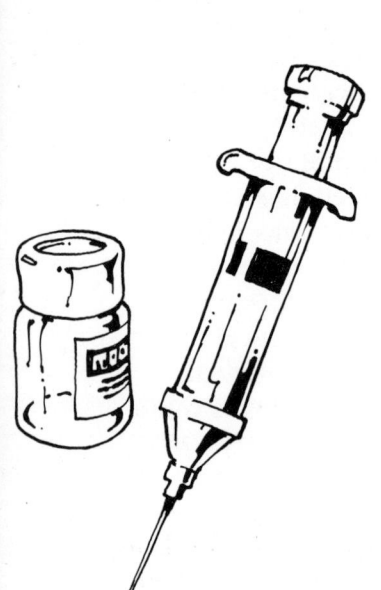

It was a happy summer. Circus audiences in the park had never before been so large and friendly. All succumbed to Ben's extraordinary charm, and Jack had never enjoyed himself so much in his life.

But nothing stays the same. After the summer, the autumn, after the brightness, the dark. Long shadows were falling. For Ben had not stopped growing. He was getting too big – much too big. It was alarming. Not to Jack, of course. He could never fear his friend. He knew that a person stayed the same inside whatever happened to his outside. He kept insisting that Ben would stop growing soon. But Ben showed no signs of stopping.

So, he was returned to the zoo, in a huge, specially built cage, and it was suggested he take a course of injections of a drug intended to stunt growth. Jack was against it. He was afraid that to tamper with Ben's nature might hurt him. But a veterinary surgeon argued that if Ben went on growing, people would become really frightened – and that what frightened them, they would eventually destroy. No one wanted that to happen, did they? So Jack gave in.

Is Jack right to give in? What do you think he should have done?

He explained the situation to Ben, whispering into his friend's enormous green ear, and Ben nodded trustingly and acceptingly.

The injections were started. At first they didn't seem to make any difference, then whatever substances that were being plugged into poor Ben began to take drastic effect. Chemical changes in the body, once made, sometimes cannot be arrested. Ben began to shrink. When he'd been reduced to a manageable size, the drug was stopped – but the shrinking continued. Ben became rapidly smaller, just as previously he'd grown rapidly bigger.

This diminishing process went on and, by the end of the winter, Ben was the same size as he had been when Jack first found him. The people who had been investigating him, making money out of him, and using him, didn't want him any more.

So one cold day, Jack called for Ben at the zoo, put him in a match-box, and took him home. This time his parents made no fuss. They were sympathetic. Their characters had seemed to improve of late.

Ben settled down to live in Jack's bedroom and Jack gave his friend complete freedom to wander at will in house and garden. He knew that however far afield Ben explored, he would always come home again . . .

But one night he didn't.

Taking a torch out into the garden, Jack searched and called. He found other caterpillars, curled up on grasses or under the shadows of leaves, but none of them had his friend's wonderfully distinctive little face.

When he went indoors again, stumbling with weariness and worry, he fell over his father's gardening shoes, which had been left in the hall because they were muddy. One shoe toppled over. Jack saw the muddied sole. There were bits of grass and leaves sticking to it. There was also a tiny squashed creature of brighter green. A squashed caterpillar? Not an ordinary caterpillar. There was a glitter of tiny gems where its head had been. Jack collected them and looked at them through his magnifying glass. Ben's teeth.

His father found him weeping over them. 'Oh, Dad, why can't you look where you're going? You trod on him and now he's dead!' sobbed Jack.

'Oh, no,' said his father, quite stricken, 'I'm so sorry! I wouldn't have had that happen for the world. But he'd become such a *little* monster, hadn't he? Such a tiny green thing.'

Jack could only weep for the loss of his friend.

Next day, a beautiful day, the beginning of spring, he buried Ben in the garden. His mother let him have a jade brooch to use as a gravestone, and told him that nothing really dies, although no one knows exactly what happens after seeming-death.

'You'll always have your memories,' she said.

To her husband, however, she confided, while Jack was still in the garden: 'Ben is better as a memory than a reality. I don't really like unusual things. Too old for them, I guess. I'm glad it's all over.'

All over? She was wrong. It was only just the beginning, for at that moment Jack was lying on his stomach on the grass and gazing at a caterpillar he'd just found nestling against the jade gravestone of Ben the First. It wasn't an ordinary caterpillar. It was looking back at him with a tiny, green human face. He could hardly believe his eyes. With trembling hands, he picked it up, put it in a match-box, took it to his room and examined it under his magnifying-glass.

It wasn't Ben, of course. Ben was dead. But it belonged to the same species and had the same gentle, almost saintly expression, as if a world of wisdom were packed into its tiny head.

'Hello, Ben the Second,' said Jack. 'Oh, I am glad to see you! Were you born the moment Ben the First died, or something like that? – like the phoenix rising from the ashes? I wish you could speak and tell me all the mysteries!'

And then, faint as the tinkle of a harebell in a summer wind, a tiny voice said: 'One day, I will.'

Rosemary Timperley

1 Why do Jack's parents think of the green thing as a 'monster'?

2 Why does the police constable not think of the green thing as a 'monster'?

3 Why do so many people make a fuss and come to see the green thing?

4 Why is Jack kind to the green thing?

Imagine you are the reporter from the local paper who goes to the zoo to find out about the green thing. You interview Jack, his mother and father, the policeman and the RSPCA man.

Write a report for your paper about the green thing.

Include everything you have found out from your interviews as well as your own description of what the green thing is like. Don't forget to make up a headline for your report and include a picture.

If this story was made into a film, it would need a poster to make people want to go and see it.

Design a poster that tells people about the film and gets them interested in it.

The green thing is unusual. At first people laugh and point at it in the zoo.

Write a story about someone or something that people treat unkindly because it is different.

Jack agrees when the RSPCA man says the best place for Ben is in the zoo. He agrees when the vet says Ben should have injections to stop him growing.

Supposing Jack had *not* agreed with either of them. What would he have said, and what would they have said?

Write down the argument he might have had with **either** the RSPCA man **or** the vet.

After Ben's death, Jack finds Ben the Second. Ben the Second can *speak*. What will Ben the Third be able to do, and Ben the Fourth?

Write the story of one of Ben's descendants.

Who killed Ben?

The suspects: Jack's mother: she never liked Ben.
The newspaper: it made use of Ben.
The circus: it used Ben to make money.
The vet: he gave Ben the drug.
The zoo: it got rid of Ben.
Jack: he didn't look after Ben properly.
Jack's father: he trod on Ben.

They are all on trial, accused of killing Ben, but whose fault was it? Were they all to blame, or was it just an accident? Your court must decide who is guilty.

You will need to work in groups of four.

1 Two of you must work out the reasons why each of the seven suspects might be to blame for Ben's death, and all the facts that prove it.

   Two of you must work out the reasons why each of the seven suspects was *not* to blame for Ben's death, and the facts which prove it.

2 When your notes are prepared and you are ready to try the suspects, ask someone from another group to come and listen to your arguments for and against each suspect. This person must listen carefully to your arguments and then decide who was to blame for Ben's death.

The dinosaur in your local museum has been vandalised. Several of its bones have been stolen. The police say that the attack happened between seven and nine o'clock last Friday evening and that three people in your class did it. They say they didn't do it. They say they were together, but doing something else at the time, and they were nowhere near the museum.

Someone who is accused of a crime can explain to the police where he was and what he was doing when he was supposed to have done the crime. This explanation is called an *alibi*. If it is true, it proves that the accused person could not have done the crime. Some alibis are truthful, but some are lies.

Choose three members of your class to be the accused people. Send them out of the classroom for ten minutes so that they can prepare their alibi. They must make sure that they all agree on their story.

You don't know whether they stole the dinosaur's bones or not, but you are going to find out. You are the investigators, and your job is to ask the three people questions to find out whether their alibi is true or false. You will know whether it's true or false, depending on whether their three stories match up or not.

First, ask one of them to come back into the classroom. Ask lots of questions and make a note of the answers. Then, keep the person in the classroom. He or she must not say anything else to anybody.

Ask the second person to come in. Ask lots more questions. Check whether what the second person says is the same as what the first person said. When you have finished the questions, keep the second person in the classroom as well.

Finally, ask the third person to come in. Do the same thing again. By the end of the third person's answers you should have a good idea whether the alibi is true or false, and whether the three of them stole the dinosaur's bones or not. If you decide that they did steal the bones, then you must also decide what punishment they deserve.

A small dragon

I've found a small dragon in the woodshed.
Think it must have come from deep inside a forest
because it's damp and green and leaves
are still reflecting in its eyes.

I fed it on many things, tried grass,
the roots of stars, hazel-nut and dandelion,
but it stared up at me as if to say, I need
foods you can't provide.

It made a nest among the coal,
not unlike a bird's but larger,
it is out of place here
and is quite silent.

If you believed in it I would come
hurrying to your house to let you share my wonder,
but I want instead to see
if you yourself will pass this way.

Brian Patten

In groups, discuss your answers to the following
questions. Make notes during your discussion, so
that you will remember all your ideas if your teacher
asks you to speak to the rest of the class, or to write
your answers down neatly.

1 Is it a real dragon in the poem?

2 If a complete stranger told you that they had found
   a dragon in a woodshed, what would you think,
   what would you do, and why?

3 If your mother told you that she had found a dragon
   in a woodshed, what would you think, what would
   you do, and why?

4 If you found a dragon in a woodshed, would it
   matter if no one believed you?

Like

Like is an important word when you are describing things, when you say one thing is *like* something else.

For example: The monster was *like* a runaway lorry.
The monster smelt *like* a barrel of sour rice pudding.
The monster's teeth were *like* rotting tree stumps.

Finish these sentences with ideas of your own:

The monster's eyes bulged *like*...
The monster's skin felt *like*...
The monster's breath smelt *like*...
The monster's roar sounded *like*...

You may be able to think of more sentences to describe a monster using *like*.

Next, in not more than 40 words describe what one of these is like:

- accidentally treading on the end of a monster's tail with your bare foot.
- reaching right under your bed for your shoe in the dark.
- being locked in a dark room and hearing a strange sound.
- walking face-first into a large spider's web.

You may have a small brother or sister, or know a small child. Write a short story that they will enjoy being scared by.

Use *like* whenever you are describing something in the story.

You could present this story as a picture book for children.

Describe the world the fish monster lives in, down in the depths. Remember to use *like*.

An alien is someone who comes from another land, a stranger.

The aliens

'How many of them are there going to be, Dad?' Terri asked, a little nervously.

'Oh, only two.' His father, Ambassador to the United Galactic Federation of Planets, tried to make his voice sound confident and reassuring.

Terri felt his mother shiver slightly. She was sitting beside him in the transit capsule as it sped along the gleaming tunnels beneath the city of Norica. Terri could sense that both his parents were rather scared about the forthcoming ordeal.

Norica was the main city of the Planet Thuron, and it held the giant Ambassadorial Centre to which every intelligent, space-travelling race in the Galaxy sent representatives. Terri's father was one of these.

New candidates to join the Federation of Planets were very rare. In fact, for centuries past, there had been none. Then suddenly an alien ship had appeared in the skies over Norica. Excitement everywhere had been intense, and the Joint Council of the Federation of Planets had immediately sent up a party of officials to interview the newcomers.

And what newcomers! Everything about them was supposed to be top-secret, but certain details had leaked out. They were an entirely alien species of people, quite unlike any ever seen before; monsters, some said. Terri felt himself growing worried at the prospect of actually seeing them in the flesh. He had begged and persuaded his parents to be taken along when he first heard that his father had been invited to the official presentation of the Aliens to the Joint Council. Now he was not so sure that he really wanted to see them for himself. His classmate Edda, daughter of the Menian Ambassador, claimed that they were too horrible to look at. Supposing they really were that dreadful . . .?

'Do you think we should have brought Terri, dear?' his mother asked anxiously. 'Isn't he a little too young?'

'Of course I'm not,' Terri interrupted scornfully, before his father had a chance to reply. 'I'm not scared of what they'll look like, Mother. Anyhow, I'm going to be an Ambassador myself one day. You have to learn to deal with all sorts of creatures.'

'That's right.' His father glanced at Terri approvingly, pressing the buttons that guided the capsule into the right tunnel. 'You can't judge any species by looks alone. Maybe they are a little weird to our way of thinking. But they've passed the first test of an advanced race; they've made it into space and reached all the way from their home planet to Thuron. So we must assume that, appearances apart, they are as civilised as we are.'

His wife was not convinced.

'Well, I hope they are as civilised as you say,' she said. 'But don't forget, they must be well behind us in space travel or it wouldn't have taken them this long to find out about Thuron. When you really think about it,' she added, 'they're practically primitives. I bet it isn't many years since they were living in caves, or whatever they have on their planet.'

It was a disturbing thought.

'But think of the Martians,' Terri argued. 'They look like huge insects and I expect everybody was frightened of them when they first arrived. But they're a perfectly reasonable race, and everyone's so used to them now that we hardly notice all those legs and feelers they have.'

'Exactly,' nodded his father. 'It's the same with the Radians. Just imagine what a shock you'd have if you saw a Radian for the first time! Two heads, all that fur, and the way they hop about instead of walking is very strange when you think about it. Yet they're generally considered to be the wisest race in the whole Galactic Federation.'

'I expect you're right,' said Terri's mother reluctantly. 'Anyway, we haven't even seen these Aliens yet. They may look quite normal.'

Their capsule was docking smoothly now in the area beneath the Assembly Building, and Terri peered eagerly out of the window to see the other Ambassadors disembarking. Most of them had arrived separately and entered the Assembly Hall by their own private escalators, since they each needed different environments and air supplies.

'What sort of atmosphere do the Aliens need, Dad?' he asked as his father climbed out of the capsule.

'I don't know, but it gave the Federation Technicians a lot of headaches to prepare it. They breathe a rather strange gas mixture.'

'Gas . . .?' Terri's mother's voice was faint, but full of foreboding.

'It's all right, dear,' the Ambassador said patiently as he helped her up the ramp and into the escalator which would take them into their own pressurised observation-booth. 'They will be kept quite separate from the rest of us. They aren't properly out of quarantine yet.'

Perhaps the Aliens had brought some dreadful plague with them, thought Terri, his flesh creeping. Or suppose they were violent? They might smash their way out of their observation-booth and run amok. He began to wonder if he could pretend a stomach-ache and be sent back – but then, Edda would laugh at him and tease him for being a scaredy-cat. He had boasted to the whole class when his father had told him that he had permission to go to the Presentation. Nobody else had been able to attend. Everybody had been so jealous, and Terri had felt really proud.

But what if he panicked when he saw the Aliens? Suppose they were as terrifying as Edda said, so ugly and repulsive that you would wake up screaming every night for a month afterwards if you even glimpsed one once?

'I may have hysterics,' his mother was saying in a very calm voice as she seated herself in the booth. 'If these Creatures are as bad as I have heard, I shan't answer for the consequences when I see them.'

His father gave her a cross look.

'Really, dear, you should try to be a little more broad-minded if only for Terri's sake,' he said. 'You'll frighten him with your silly talk. I tell you they're not horrible to look at. They are probably very pleasant Creatures.'

Terri's mother sniffed, unconvinced. 'Just as long as they behave. What is that ghastly mess spread out on the table down there?'

Terri adjusted the viewing screen in front of them so that it scanned in close-up across the area where the Reception Committee was gathered, waiting to greet the Aliens formally.

'Food,' his father said shortly.

'Food?' Terri and his mother exchanged horrified looks. 'That – sickening heap of rotting garbage? Do you mean they *eat* that?' His mother's voice had risen an octave.

'Apparently. The Federation Corps is very accurate when it comes to duplicating these things.'

Terri thought that even his father did not sound too sure; as for himself, his stomach turned over at the disgusting sight. A lot of sickening, chopped-up dead creatures and different kinds of plants, most of it partly burned for some reason, was spread out on the table below. Whatever could the Aliens be like, to eat such a foul-looking mess?

He suddenly became aware that all the lights in the vast Hall were dimming, except for those in the Reception Booth. All the Ambassadors craned forwards for their first glimpses of the Aliens. Voices died away into silence, and then through the speaker Terri heard the president of the Council begin his address of welcome.

His mouth dried and he tensed up completely as the door at the rear of the Hall slowly opened. A brilliant light danced down to illuminate the Aliens emerging through it. Please, please, Terri thought desperately, don't let me make a fool of myself. Don't let me scream . . .

The Aliens came into the light. They were certainly odd – one was pink, and one was brown, and they only had two flat eyes each at the front of their round heads; but they were not as awful as all that.

Terri shot his mother a look of relief, and slowly relaxed. He was already imagining what he would say to Edda in class tomorrow, something really offhand and casual:

'Oh, they're O.K., Edda, they don't frighten me. Earthmen? I can take 'em or leave 'em.'

And Terri settled back into his chair, comfortably coiling his seven tentacles beneath him.

Roger Malisson

1 Terri's father says the Aliens breathe a 'rather strange gas mixture'. *What is it?*

2 'A lot of sickening, chopped-up dead creatures and different kinds of plants, most of it partly burned for some reason . . .' *What is it?*

3 One of the Aliens is pink, and one is brown. *What are they?*

At the end of the story we learn that Terri has seven tentacles instead of legs. He must be as strange to the 'Aliens' as the 'Aliens' are to him. Of course, even though he calls them 'Aliens', they are not aliens to us.

The Aliens came into the hall where the reception committee was waiting for them. Imagine that you were one of the Aliens. Describe what it was like, coming through the door and seeing all the creatures waiting. Describe what happened to you after that.

Draw a picture of either Terri, or one of the other creatures waiting to meet the Aliens.

All the planets in the universe are members of The United Galactic Federation Of Planets. The Federation Guidebook has pictures in it of all the creatures from each different planet and descriptions of them all. It has details of where they live, what they eat, what their habits are, and examples of how they speak.

Design some pages from the Guidebook.

You could include some of the different creatures from the story and the creature on the cover of this book. If you work in pairs or in groups you will be able to make a complete Guidebook.

There are lots of strange creatures on the planet Earth. Look in your library for books on animals and birds. Find the ones that seem strangest to you, then draw them and write down why they are so strange.

If you get stuck you could look up these:
    the trap-door spider
    the giant armadillo
    the duck-billed platypus
    the dwarf anteater

BEAUTY AND THE BEAST

You may know the story of Beauty and the Beast. Look at these pictures from the story, drawn by three different artists.

Which do you think is the ugliest beast, and which is the most beautiful girl?

Write a description of the beast and the girl you have chosen. Then explain why you chose each of them.

'It may have looked ugly, but it had a heart of gold . . .' Describe a creature that most people thought was ugly, but which turned out to be beautiful in its own way.

What do you think is the most beautiful thing in the world? Write down your answer and explain why.

Ask other people the same question and write down their answers and their explanations under yours.

In groups, make a list of ten things in the world that everyone in your group agrees are beautiful.

On your own, write a poem, describing one of the beautiful things your group chose.

Make a collage of pictures of beautiful things and ugly things. Include words which describe the pictures you've chosen.

Read the following poem. The meanings of seven
words in it are explained at the side of the poem.

The trap

The first night that the monster lurched
Out of the forest on all fours,
He saw its shadow in his dream
Circle the house, as though it searched
For one it loved or hated. Claws
On gravel and a rabbit's scream
Ripped the fabric of his dream.

Waking between dark and dawn
And sodden sheets, his reason quelled◊   ◊stopped
The shadow and the nightmare sound.
The second night it crossed the lawn
A brute voice in the darkness yelled.
He struggled up, woke raving, found
His wall-flowers trampled to the ground.

When rook wings beckoned the shadows back
He took his rifle down, and stood
All night against the leaded glass.
The moon ticked round. He saw the black
Elm-skeletons in the doomsday wood,
The sailing and the failing stars
And red coals dropping between bars.

The third night such a putrid◊ breath   ◊rotten
Fouled, flared his nostrils, that he turned,
Turned, but could not lift, his head.
A coverlet as thick as death
Oppressed◊ him: he crawled out: discerned◊   ◊weighed down
Across the door his watchdog, dead.   ◊saw
'Build a trap,' the neighbours said.

All that day he built his trap
With metal jaws and a spring as thick
As the neck of a man. One touch
Triggered the hanging teeth: jump, snap,
And lightning guillotined the stick
Thrust in its throat. With gun and torch
He set his engine in the porch.

The fourth night in their beds appalled[◊]   ◊frightened
His neighbours heard the hunting roar
Mount, mount to an exultant[◊] shriek.   ◊delighted
At daybreak timidly they called
His name, climbed through the splintered door
And found him sprawling in the wreck,
Naked, with a severed[◊] neck.   ◊cut through

Jon Stallworthy

The poem describes what happened each night. It
also tells us a little about what the man did in the
daytime.

Read the poem again carefully. If you can, work out
what happened on each of the four nights and the
three days.

Then, write down your answers to the following
questions:
1 What happened on the second night?
2 What did the man do before it got dark on the
next evening?
3 What did the man do on the third day?
4 What happened on the fourth night?
5 What happened on the last morning?
6 Is it a real monster?

Choose one line or a group of lines from the poem as
the title for a picture. Your picture does not have to
show what happens in the poem. You may want to
draw something else to go with your title.

Some people believe that our dreams can tell us what is going to happen in the future. Here is a page from a book that tries to explain what our dreams mean. Look at what it says about a monster in a dream.

MYSTIC DREAM BOOK

MONEY. — To dream that you pay or give Money to other people is a fortunate omen; prosperity awaits you. To dream that you receive Money also foretells personal success, but due to hard work. To find Money in your dream is not so fortunate, however — there will be some sudden advancement or success, but it will prove disappointing. It is a very bad sign if you dream that you borrow Money, either from a friend or from a moneylender.

MONK. — As with others connected with the Church, this is an omen of disappointment and trouble.

MONSTER. — To see a Monster in the sea is not good; but out of the sea, good luck.

MOON. — This dream depends upon the circumstances. If the Moon is bright and shines clearly, free from cloud, it foretells success in love, personal happiness. If the Moon is clouded over, it shows ill-health, or some other interruption to your comfort and enjoyment. A New Moon is fortunate for business; a Full Moon for love affairs. See also **COMET.**

MORNING. — An excellent sign. Your fate is protected from evil. Be confident.

MOSS. — Take care of your correspondence. Write guardedly; seal and post carefully. Someone has an attraction towards you which will soon be expressed.

MOTH or **BUTTERFLY.** — A warning of rivals who will harm you if you are not careful in your speech and actions. Expect quarrels with your lover, husband, or wife. To those who employ others it is a sign that they are not being served faithfully.

MOTHER. — To dream that you see your Mother and converse with her is a very favourable omen.

84

Dreaming about a monster 'out of the sea' did not bring good luck to the man in the poem. So what do you think his dream tells us? What should he have done? Write down what you think his dream meant.

Ask other people about their dreams and write down what they tell you. See if you can work out what each dream means and write down your explanation next to the dream.

You could work with a group of friends on this and make a book about dreams and their meanings.

'The trap' is like a nightmare that comes true. Imagine you are babysitting for a small child. The child wakes up from a bad dream thinking there is a monster somewhere in the room. You must convince the child that it was only a dream.

Write down the conversation you have with the child about the nightmare and the monster. You could write this as a play or a story.

This extract from Maurice Sendak's picture book of
the same name is for reading aloud and acting. You
will need to work in groups.

Where the wild things are

The night Max wore his wolf suit and made mischief of one kind
and another
his mother called him 'WILD THING!'
and Max said 'I'LL EAT YOU UP!'
so he was sent to bed without eating anything.
That very night in Max's room a forest grew
and grew –
and grew until his ceiling hung with vines
and the walls became the world all around
and an ocean tumbled by with a private boat for Max
and he sailed off through night and day
and in and out of weeks
and almost over a year
to where the wild things are.
And when he came to the place where the wild things are
they roared their terrible roars and gnashed their terrible teeth
and rolled their terrible eyes and showed their terrible claws
till Max said 'BE STILL!'
and tamed them with a magic trick
of staring into all their yellow eyes without blinking once
and they were frightened and called him the most wild thing of all
and made him king of all wild things.
'And now,' cried Max, 'let the wild rumpus start!'

'Now stop!' Max said and sent the wild things off to bed
without their supper. And Max the king of all wild things was lonely
and wanted to be where someone loved him best of all.
Then all around from far away across the world
he smelled good things to eat
so he gave up being king of where the wild things are.
But the wild things cried, 'Oh please don't go –
we'll eat you up – we love you so!'
And Max said, 'No!'
The wild things roared their terrible roars and gnashed their terrible
teeth
and rolled their terrible eyes and showed their terrible claws

but Max stepped into his private boat and waved good-bye
and smiled back over a year
and in and out of weeks
and through a day
and into the night of his very own room
where he found his supper waiting for him
and it was still hot.

Maurice Sendak

Here is one way to act out the extract. Decide which of you is going to read aloud the parts of the extract which tell the story. Who is going to be Max? Who is going to be Max's mother? Who are going to be the wild things? What about the forest growing in Max's room, and the wild things gnashing their terrible teeth?

Use these suggestions if you think they will help you. Be sure to act out as much of the extract as you possibly can.

RIDDLES

Here are two riddles. What are the answers?

It has wings and breathes fire.
Its name rhymes with wagon.
What is it?

He's always drinking blood.
He eats necks to nothing.
Who is he?

Write some riddles to try out on your friends. You could also write out some riddles that you already know.

THE MACHINE MONSTER

You may have heard of Frankenstein. Frankenstein was not a monster. He was a doctor. He collected parts of human bodies and stuck them all together to make one new, living creature. Unfortunately this creature was so strong that soon Dr Frankenstein could no longer control it. It killed people. Frankenstein had created a monster.

A similar thing happens in the following very short story. Read it carefully. You will probably need to read it at least twice.

Imagine a world in the future. People are trying to get all the knowledge in the whole universe into one machine . . .

Answer

Dwar Ev ceremoniously soldered the final connection with gold. The eyes of a dozen television cameras watched him and the subether bore throughout the universe a dozen pictures of what he was doing.

He straightened and nodded to Dwar Reyn, then moved to a position beside the switch that would complete the contact when he threw it. The switch that would connect, all at once, all of the monster computing machines of all the populated planets in the universe – ninety-six billion planets – into the supercircuit that would connect them all into one supercalculator, one cybernetics machine that would combine all the knowledge of all the galaxies.

Dwar Reyn spoke briefly to the watching and listening trillions. Then after a moment's silence he said, 'Now, Dwar Ev.'

Dwar Ev threw the switch. There was a mighty hum, the surge of power from ninety-six billion planets. Lights flashed and quieted along the miles-long panel.

Dwar Ev stepped back and drew a deep breath. 'The honour of asking the first question is yours, Dwar Reyn.'

'Thank you,' said Dwar Reyn. 'It shall be a question which no single cybernetics machine has been able to answer.'

He turned to face the machine. 'Is there a God?'

The mighty voice answered without hesitation, without the clicking of a single relay.

'Yes, NOW there is a God.'

Sudden fear flashed on the face of Dwar Ev. He leaped to grab the switch.

A bolt of lightning from the cloudless sky struck him down and fused the switch shut.

Fredric Brown

1 In not more than two sentences, explain what happens in the story.

2 Explain why this story is similar to the story of Dr Frankenstein and the monster.

This story is very short. What do you think happened next? Continue the story.

Imagine you are a television or a radio commentator, watching Dwar Ev solder the final connection.

Tape your commentary on the events as they happen in this story.

Make everything sound very exciting. You may need to add sound effects. You could continue your commentary on what happens after the story has ended.

The machine in the story is accidentally turned into a monster. Draw your own imaginary machine monster. Remember to give it a name.

Write a story, with lots of detail, about a machine that gets out of control.

In groups of three, or six, read the poem aloud to yourselves. Each person could be in charge of one or two verses. You could tape your group's reading, adding plenty of sound effects, or you could act out the poem for the rest of the class.

Poem

In the stump of the old tree, where the heart has rotted out, there is a hole the length of a man's arm, and a dank pool at the bottom of it where the rain gathers, and the old leaves turn into lacy skeletons. But do not put your hand down to see, because

in the stumps of old trees, where the hearts have rotted out, there are holes the length of a man's arm, and dank pools at the bottom where the rain gathers and old leaves turn to lace, and the beak of a dead bird gapes like a trap. But do not put your hand down to see, because

in the stumps of old trees with rotten hearts, where the rain gathers and the laced leaves and the dead bird like a trap, there are holes the length of a man's arm, and in every crevice of the rotten wood grow weasel's eyes like molluscs, their lids open and shut with the tide. But do not put your hand down to see, because

in the stumps of old trees where the rain gathers and the trapped leaves and the beak, and the laced weasel's eyes, there are holes the length of a man's arm, and at the bottom a sodden bible written in the language of rooks. But do not put your hand down to see, because

in the stumps of old trees where the hearts have rotted out there are holes the length of a man's arm where the weasels are trapped and the letters of the rook language are laced on the sodden leaves, and at the bottom there is a man's arm. But do not put your hand down to see, because

in the stumps of old trees where the hearts have rotted out there are deep holes and dank pools where the rain gathers, and if you ever put your hand down to see, you can wipe it in the sharp grass till it bleeds, but you'll never want to eat with it again.

Hugh Sykes Davies

34

Carefully draw the inside of one of the tree stumps the way you imagine it, using *all* the details mentioned in the poem.

Here are some of the important words the writer uses:

leaves crevice dead bird holes face hand skeletons bible holes rain weasel's eyes rooks heart pool trap tree stump arm

In the poem he twists these words into lots of different combinations and sentences, seeing how they sound.

See if you can do the same thing to describe an old, abandoned building. Use these instructions to help you:

1. Write down ten words to do with the building.
2. Make them into lots of different sentences.
3. Cross out the sentences you don't like and keep the good ones.
4. Write out the sentences as a poem. (You may need to do some more crossing out and changing.)
5. You could read out your poem to the rest of the class or to your friends. They may have some good ideas you could use for a title.
6. Write your poem out neatly.

School monsters

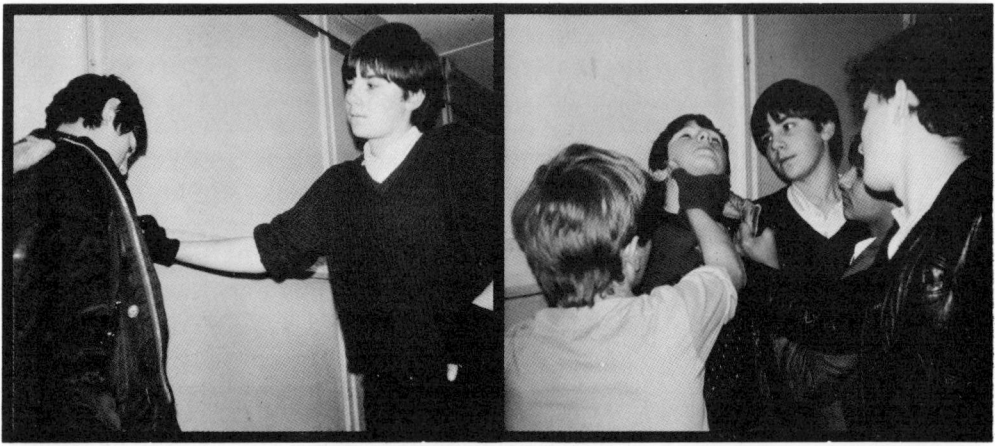

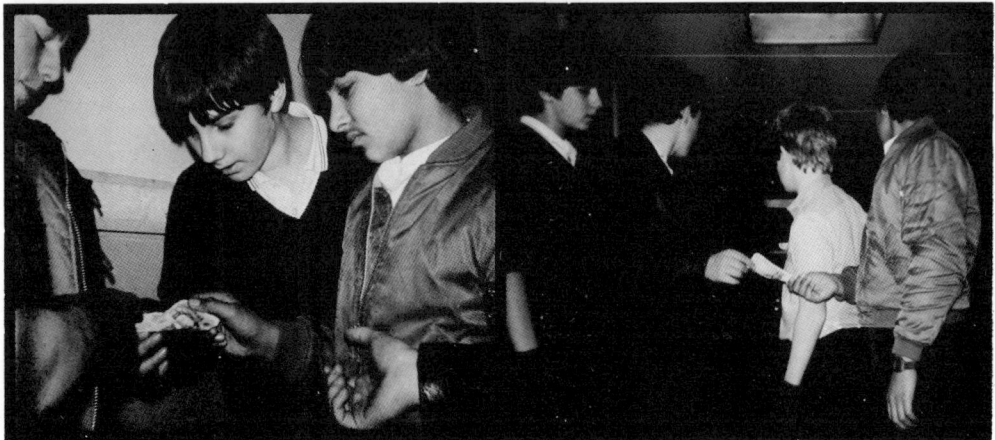

'As I walked to my classroom, I saw them coming down the corridor towards me. They called them the school monsters. Everyone knew they were bullies. I couldn't go back because they'd seen me . . .'

Getting bullied is one of the nastiest things that can happen to you in school. It can happen in lots of ways. The photo story on the opposite page shows only one of these ways.

You will need to work in small groups, and make these three lists:
1 A list of reasons why people get bullied.
2 A list of all the different ways in which people get bullied.
3 A list of reasons why people become bullies.

Next, using all three of your lists for ideas, work out a play about someone who gets bullied. Don't forget to decide where the bullying is going to happen.

When you have finished working on your play with your group, write a short description on your own of what happened in the play. Make sure you include answers to these questions:
Why was the victim picked on?
What happened to the victim?
What were the bullies like?

What should be done about bullying?

Think carefully about these three examples of what can happen in school, and write down your advice for each one.

'She was always waiting for me in the morning before school started, and unless I gave her something, she'd make fun of me all day.'

Explain what you would do if you were getting bullied.

'He was the untidiest boy in the class. The others kept teasing him about his clothes, saying he smelt and saying things about his mum.'

Explain what you would do if you knew someone who was getting bullied.

'She was new and I couldn't get anyone in the class even to talk to her. Eventually she started missing school.'

Explain what you think this teacher should do.

Profile: Bert 'n' Bertha

A profile contains a lot of important details about a person. If you read all the details you end up with a good picture of what the person is like.

Bert Bully is a typical school bully. Bertha Bully is his twin sister. Copy out this profile plan onto your own paper and fill in all the details from your own imagination, either for Bert, or for Bertha.

You will need to draw in the photograph, or cut one out of a magazine or newspaper, or use an old one from home. You may be able to think of more details to add.

PROFILE

NAME:
PHOTOGRAPH:

HEIGHT:
WEIGHT:
FAVOURITE SCHOOL SUBJECT:
FAVOURITE PLACE IN SCHOOL:
FAVOURITE T.V. PROGRAMME:
FAVOURITE SPORT:
FAVOURITE CLOTHES TO WEAR:
FAVOURITE FOOD:
FAVOURITE DRINK:
FAVOURITE FOOTBALL TEAM:
FAVOURITE FAMOUS PERSON:
FAVOURITE TORTURE:
DISLIKES:

INDOOR HOBBIES:

OUTDOOR HOBBIES:

BEST MOMENTS IN LIFE SO FAR:

HOPES FOR THE FUTURE:

Tell the story of one of Bert or Bertha's nasty adventures. Draw it as a strip cartoon, or write it as a story.

Write a guide, explaining how to do one of these three things:
- How To Be A Successful Bully
- How To Stop Yourself Getting Bullied
- How To Be A Bully's Best Friend

At the back of your guide make a list of any words or phrases to do with bullying which might be hard for someone else to understand. Explain each word or phrase carefully.

Death's party

Death sent them all invitations to his party, all the monsters who had made people's lives miserable. Mr Greedy, Anger and Jealousy were invited. So were Bert and Bertha Bully, Count Dracula, Prejudice, Bighead, and all the others. Enough was enough, Death thought. They'd made people unhappy for centuries and now it was time for them to go. Each one would die in a different way. Death had decided on a suitable end for each of them. They would die one by one at his party. Mr Greedy would be no problem. Death had already ordered five hundred cream cakes . . .

Describe what happened at the party and the way each of Death's guests died. Make sure the way they die fits the sort of monster they are.

Brave Molly

A little girl was once caught in a thunderstorm. The day grew dark, and the wind started to blow, and suddenly a fork of lightning streaked across the sky and a great clap of thunder rolled all around her. Poor Molly trembled with fright, and she wished she were back at home with her mother. Then it started to rain. Such a cloudburst it was! The heavens just opened up and down came the rain in great big drops the size of your fist.

In the distance, Molly could see a little hut, so she ran up to it and, finding the door open, she slipped into the gloomy inside. No sooner had she shut the door than a deep growling voice said: 'Grrrrr! Who are you?'

Molly looked around her, but the inside of the hut was quite dark, and she couldn't see anyone.

'P-p-p-please . . . my name's M-M-M-Molly,' she said. 'Who are you?'

'Grrrrr! I'm a Terrible Monster – that's who!' said the voice.

Just then a bolt of lightning lit up the inside of the hut for a fraction of a second and, in that moment, Molly saw a huge black shape crouching against the far end of the hut. 'Ohhhhh!' she cried.

'What's the matter?' growled the Terrible Monster. 'Frightened, are you?'

'Indeed I am,' said Molly. 'You're as black as coal, as big as a house and covered in hair.'

'And I've got a terrible roar,' said the Monster. 'AAAAAAAARRRRRRRGH!'

Poor Molly fell over backwards in her fright. And the thunder crashed over their heads, and another flash of lightning lit up the Monster, and Molly could see that he had great black claws and glowing eyes and huge yellow teeth.

'Pretty frightening, huh?' bellowed the Monster.

'Oh y-y-y-yes!' cried Molly.

'*And* I'm as strong as two hundred oxen!' he cried and, as the lightning flashed, Molly saw the Monster rear up on his legs and throw the roof of the hut high into the air.

'Oh . . . please don't!' cried Molly, as the rain started to pour down on her and the thunder crashed.

'*And* I eat little girls for my supper!' roared the Monster. And he bent down and put one glowing eye right up against poor Molly, and said: 'How about *that?*'

'Well,' Molly thought to herself, 'it's no use being frightened. If he's going to eat me – he's going to eat me.' So she picked up her satchel and hit that Monster right on the nose. And do you know what happened? Well, the Monster didn't pick her up in his huge claws, and he didn't gobble her up with his great yellow teeth. Do you know what he did? First he turned green, then he turned black and then he turned bright pink, and a bunch of flowers grew out of the top of his head.

'Why! You're not a frightening monster at all!' cried Molly.

'Aren't I?' said the Monster.

'No!' said Molly, and a beautiful ribbon tied in a bow suddenly appeared right round the Monster's middle. And Molly took hold of the ribbon and pulled it and the Monster opened up and inside was a little rabbit who looked very frightened and said: 'Oh please! Don't put me in a pie!'

And Brave Molly said: 'I won't put you in a pie this time, but don't go around trying to frighten little children in future.'

'No . . . I promise,' said the rabbit, and scuttled off out of the hut.

And just then the sky cleared and the sun came out, and Brave Molly set off home again, and she didn't meet another monster all the rest of the way.

Terry Jones

1 Why does the monster show off so much?
2 Why doesn't the monster eat Molly when she hits it with her satchel?
3 Why is there a rabbit inside the monster?
4 What is the story about Molly and the monster trying to tell us?

Write a story of your own, trying to say the same thing as this one, but in a completely different way with a completely different story.

Re-write the story of Brave Molly as if you were the monster. Describe your feelings, what you did when Molly came into the hut, how you felt when she hit you on the nose, and what happened at the end.

Turn the story of Brave Molly into a cartoon story, with no words, just drawings to show what happens. Use no more than ten drawings and include as many details from the story as you can.

VAMPIRES

A vampire is a dead body that comes alive again at night time. It has sharp fangs, and sucks the blood out of living people when they are asleep. This blood keeps the vampire alive. When morning comes, the vampire goes back to its grave.

In certain places, people think that unless you put money into the mouth of a dead body when it is being buried, then the ghost of the dead body will come out of the grave and will be a vampire.

Garlic helps keep vampires away, but the way to kill a vampire is to drive a wooden stake through its heart.

The most famous vampire was Count Dracula. He used to invite people to his castle in the mountains of Transylvania so that he could attack them and drink their blood.

Imagine that you are a detective, and you have been asked to find out whether the rumours about Count Dracula are true.

Either, write the diary you kept each day during the investigation, or, write a description of the most frightening part of the investigation.

The monster of the loch

Legend tells of a water horse haunting the lonely lochs of Scotland, an evil spirit that lured weary travellers to their deaths.

The outside world did not hear of the Loch Ness Monster until 1933, when a main road was built, linking the loch with the rest of Scotland. A local newspaper then told of the 'STRANGE SPECTACLE ON LOCH NESS!' and since then, reports of the sightings have increased.

Over 4,000 people have said that they have seen the Loch Ness Monster.

What does it look like?

This photograph was taken at Loch Ness in 1934. Many people think it is of the monster.

  # An eye-witness account

'I was with my two brothers and my younger sister Lizzie, who was in the pram. We were waiting for some friends and were passing the time by skimming stones across the water when we heard this awful crackling in the trees on the other side of the little bay.

It must have been something awfully big, we thought; and of course we had been warned not to go near the loch by our grandparents.

So we sat for a while and this crackling seemed to be coming nearer and nearer, and then, suddenly, this big thing appeared out of the trees and started to move down the beach to the water. It had a huge body and its movement as it came out of the trees was like a caterpillar. I would say it was a good twenty feet long – what we saw of it. It was the colour of an elephant, and it seemed to have rather a shiny skin. Under it we saw two short, round feet at the front and it lurched to one side and put one foot into the water and then the other one. We didn't wait to see the end of it coming out of the bushes – we got too big a fright. When we got home we were all sick and couldn't take our tea. I'll never forget it.'

Mrs Margaret Cameron, September 1971

 Imagine you are camping by Loch Ness with some friends. You are on your own one evening, when you see something moving close to the shore. You look carefully and suddenly you realise what it is . . .

Continue the story of what you saw and what happened. You could include a drawing of what you saw.

For this game you will need a dice. If you don't have one, you can write the numbers on the sides of a pencil, and roll the pencil to get your scores. Each player will also need a counter. You can make counters out of rough paper, with your initials on them.

Can you invent another game to find another monster?

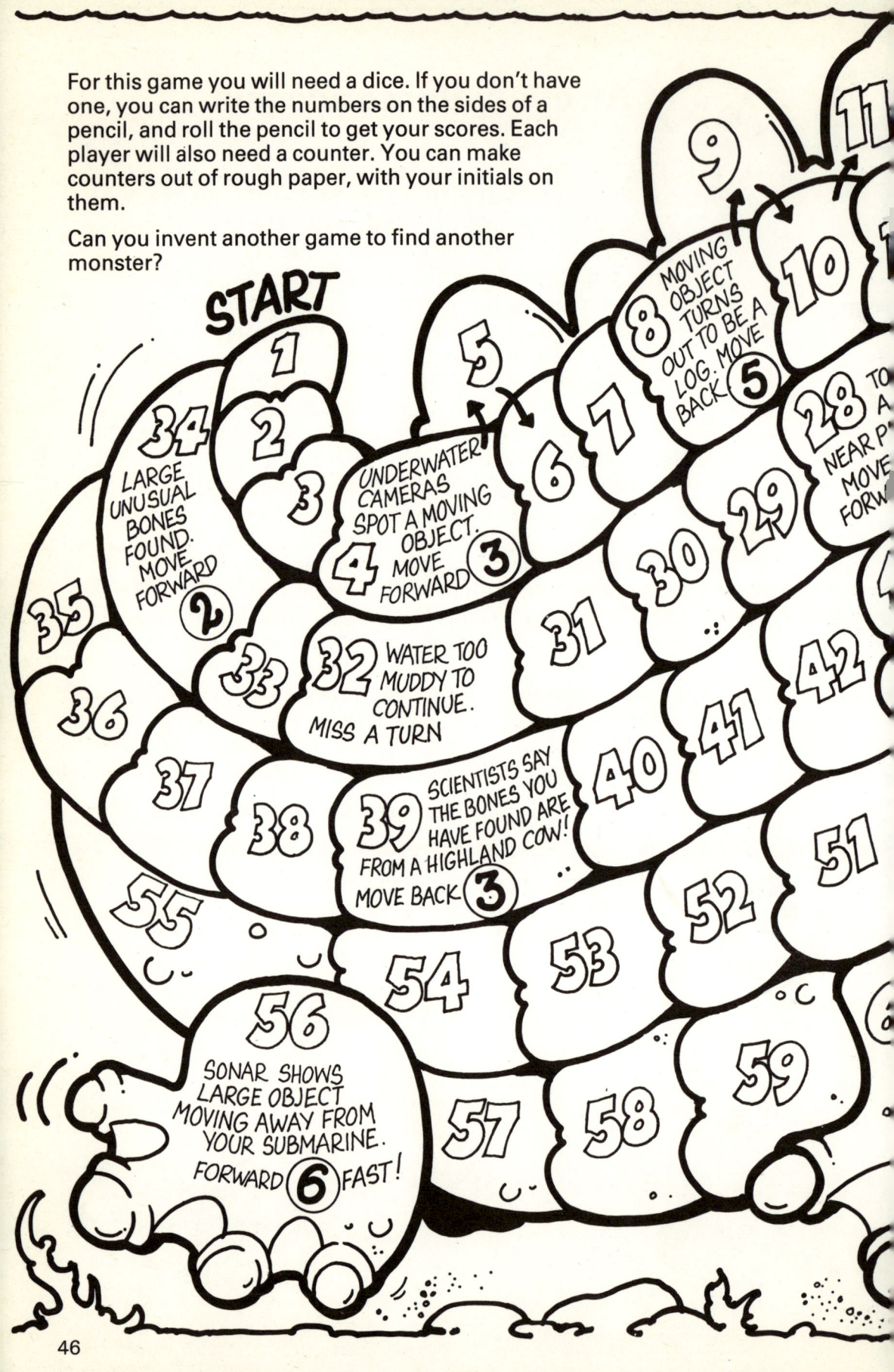

START

1
2
3
4 UNDERWATER CAMERAS SPOT A MOVING OBJECT. MOVE FORWARD 3
5
6
7
8 MOVING OBJECT TURNS OUT TO BE A LOG. MOVE BACK 5
9
10
11
28 TO A NEAR P MOVE FORW
29
30
31
32 WATER TOO MUDDY TO CONTINUE. MISS A TURN
33
34 LARGE UNUSUAL BONES FOUND. MOVE FORWARD 2
35
36
37
38
39 SCIENTISTS SAY THE BONES YOU HAVE FOUND ARE FROM A HIGHLAND COW! MOVE BACK 3
40
41
42
51
52
53
54
55
56 SONAR SHOWS LARGE OBJECT MOVING AWAY FROM YOUR SUBMARINE. FORWARD 6 FAST!
57
58
59

Acknowledgements

For permission to reprint copyright material the publishers wish to thank: George Allen & Unwin for 'A small dragon' by Brian Patten (© 1969 Brian Patten) from *Notes to the hurrying man*; The Bodley Head for 'Where the wild things are' from the book of the same name by Maurice Sendak (© 1963 Maurice Sendak); Fredric Brown for 'Answer', reprinted by permission of the author and the author's agents, Scott Meredith Literary Agency, Inc., 845 Third Avenue, New York, New York 10022; Wm Collins Sons & Co Ltd for 'The aliens' by Roger Malisson (© 1975 Roger Malisson) from *Second Armada Book of Monsters* edited by Ronald Chetwynd-Hayes; Michael Joseph Ltd for 'Brave Molly' from *Fairy Tales* by Terry Jones (© 1981 Terry Jones) published by Pavilion Books Ltd in association with Michael Joseph; Oxford University Press for 'The trap' from *Out of bounds* by John Stallworthy (© 1963 Oxford University Press); Harvey Unna & Stephen Durbridge Ltd for 'The green thing' by Rosemary Timperley (© 1975 Rosemary Timperley and her agent Harvey Unna) from *Second Armada Book of Monsters* edited by Ronald Chetwynd-Hayes ; Benedict Luxmoore.

For permission to reproduce illustrations the publishers wish to thank: Collection Haags Gemeentemuseum – The Hague for 'Three worlds' (page 17) and 'Stars' (page 23) by M. C. Escher; William Heinemann Ltd for 'At the dead of night, in came the Welsh Giant' by Arthur Rackham (page 29), from *The Allies Fairy Book*; The Kobal Collection (page 43); Ladybird Books Ltd, Loughborough (page 25) from the Ladybird book *Beauty and the Beast*; London *Daily Mail* (page 44); David Richardson (page 35).

The publishers have made every effort to trace the copyright-holders but if they have inadvertently failed to acknowledge any copyright, they will be pleased to make the necessary arrangement at the first opportunity.

Additional illustrations by John Plumb

ISBN 0 340 25129 8

First published 1985

Copyright© 1985 Richard Haycraft and Nicholas Luxmoore

Photoset by Rowland Phototypesetting Ltd,
Bury St Edmunds, Suffolk
Printed in Hong Kong for
Hodder and Stoughton Educational,
a division of Hodder and Stoughton Ltd,
Mill Road, Dunton Green, Sevenoaks, Kent
by Colorcraft Ltd